The Tynese Elves Coloring Book

Available from Amazon.com, CreateSpace.com, and other retail outlets

Welcome!

But Don't Be So Serious…

Allow your cares to drift away while coloring each enchanting scene, let your imagination flow …to wander and wonder. *Well, you could at least try, can't ya?*

Imagine yourself being on the first crossing of a mighty river in a giant's goblet! (a coffee cup on a creek). Or, among a group of elves engaged in the always dangerous work of excavating carrots (a favorite food of the elves). Or, dodging others in the frantic spectacle of busy cooking preparations for a feast.
Coloring enthusiasts of any age will enjoy coloring these whimsical, illustrated scenes featuring the Tynese Elves.

A list of the scenes:

- To Market
- Carrot Fields
- Giant's Fearsome Machine
- Old Rat Hunter
- Daffodils For Dye
- Curious Minds
- Carrot Trading
- New River Ferry
- Carrot Poaching
- Starting To Rain
- Finding Time
- Before Crows Come
- Hectic Feast Day
- Rainy Day
- Haste

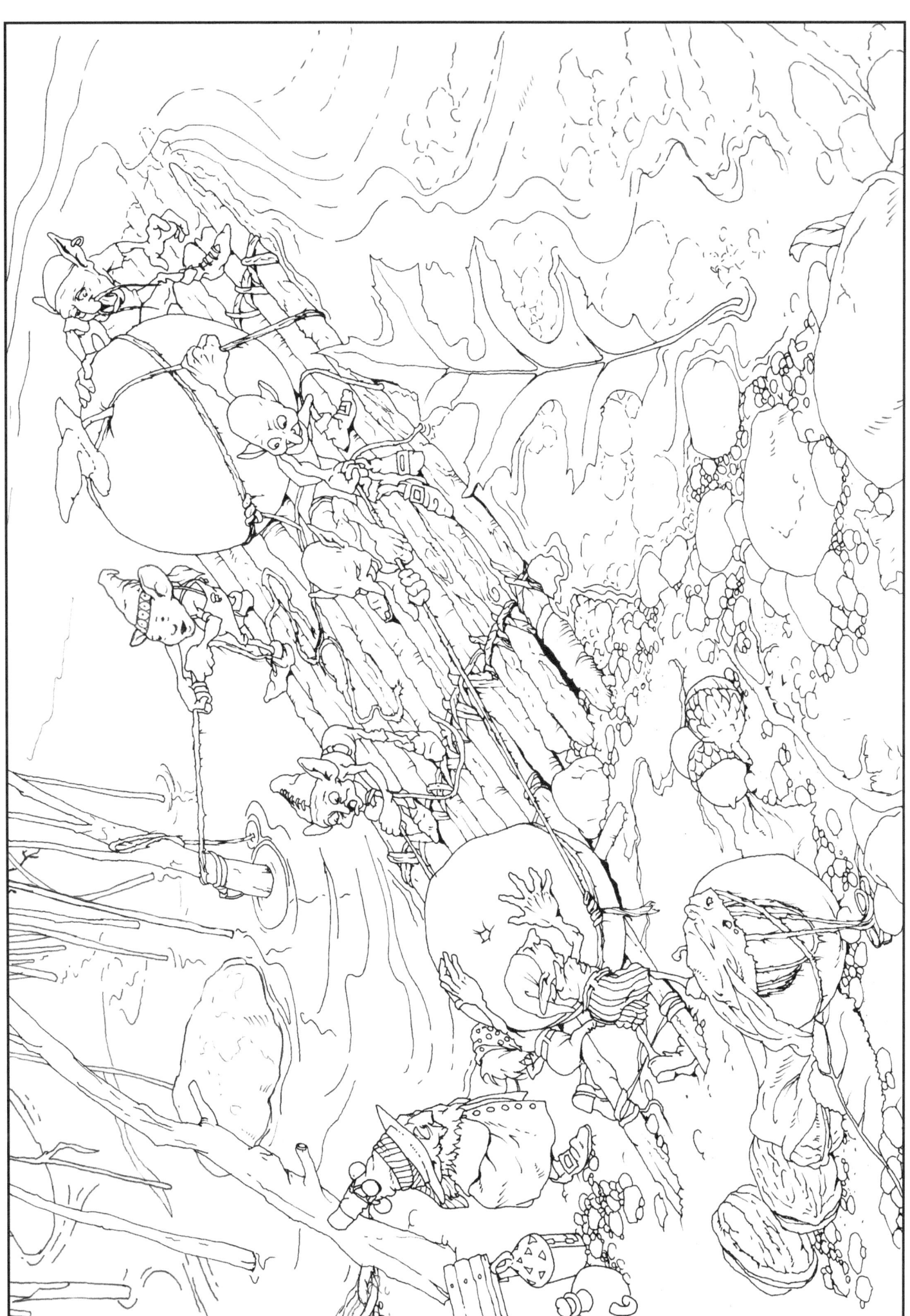

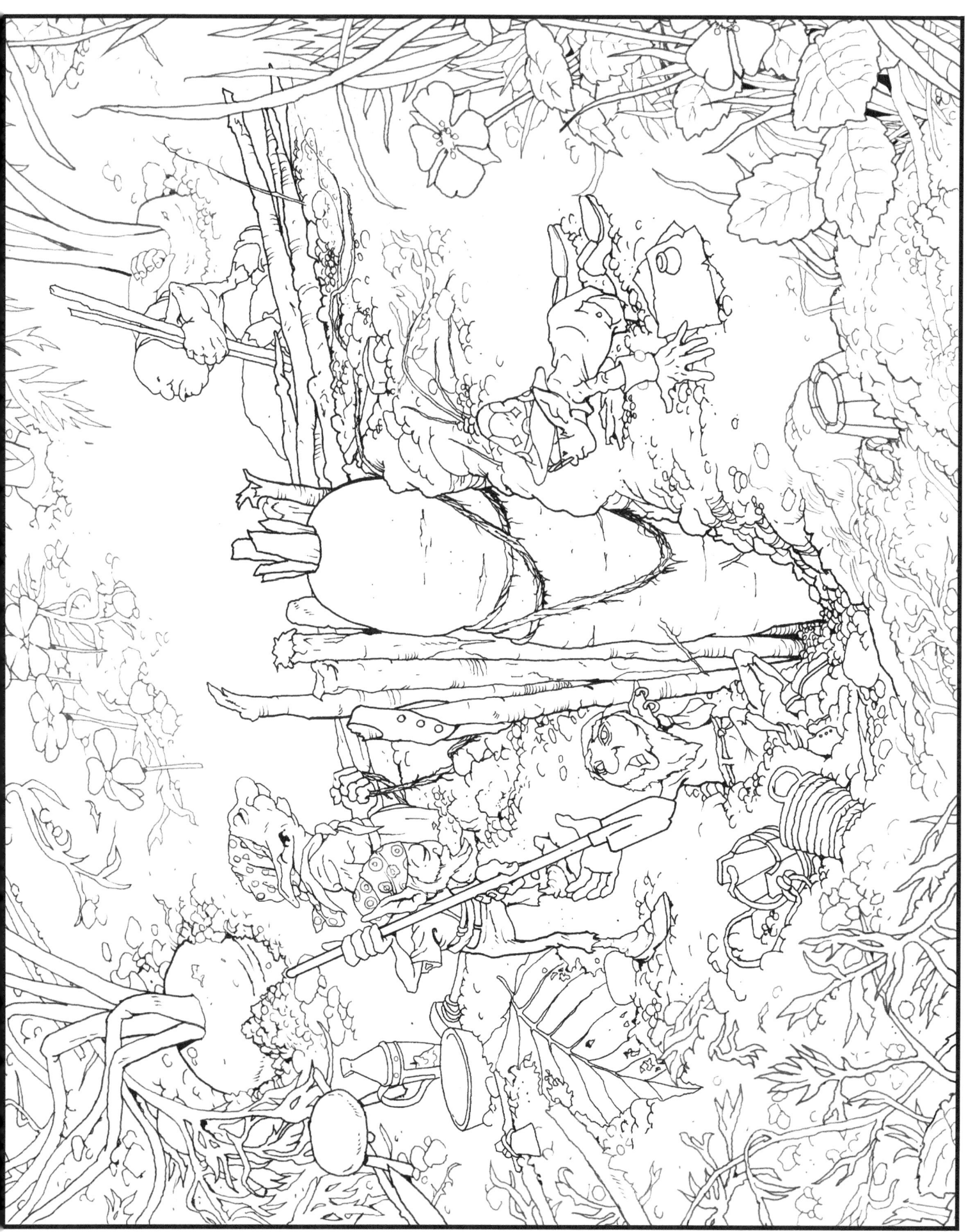

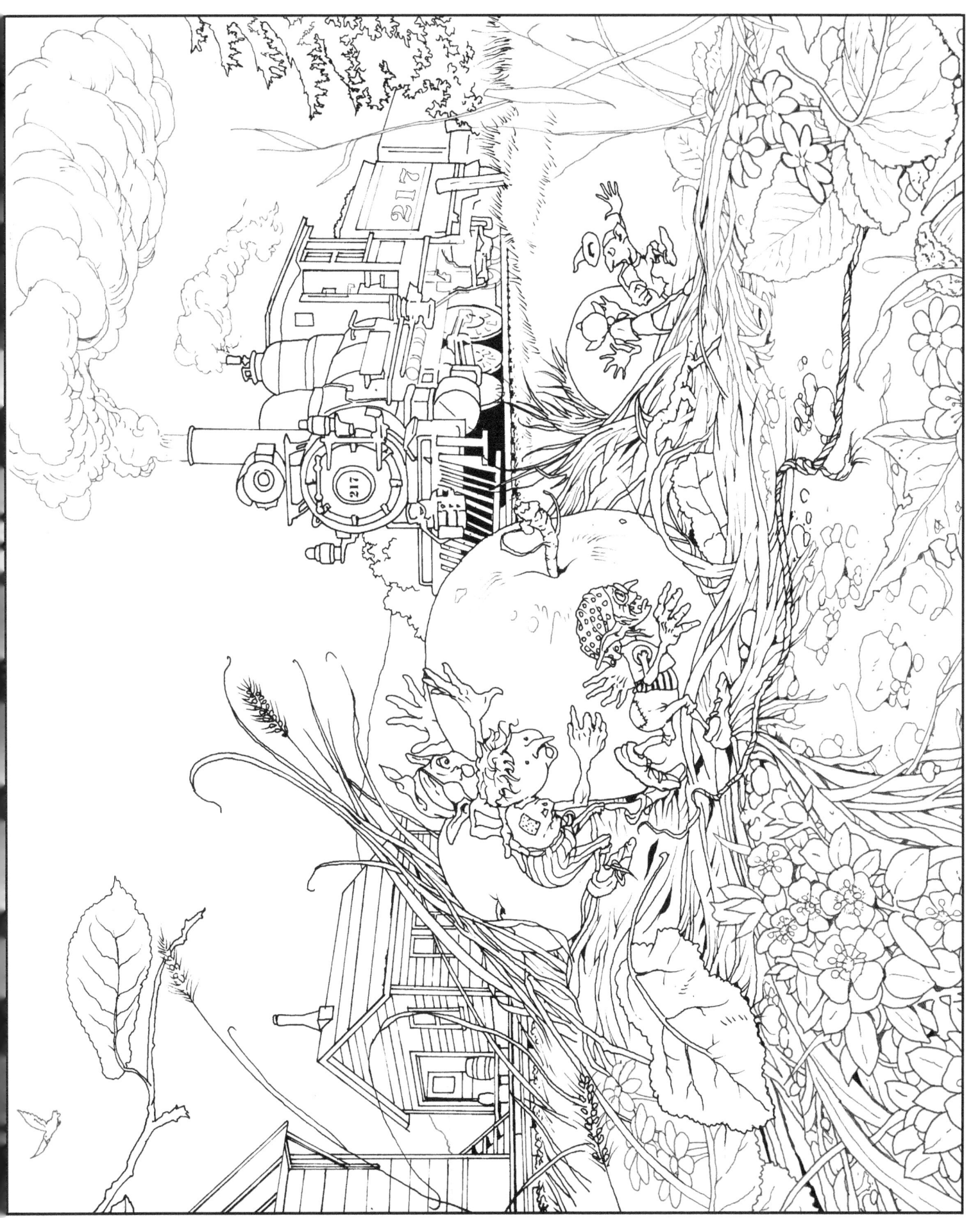

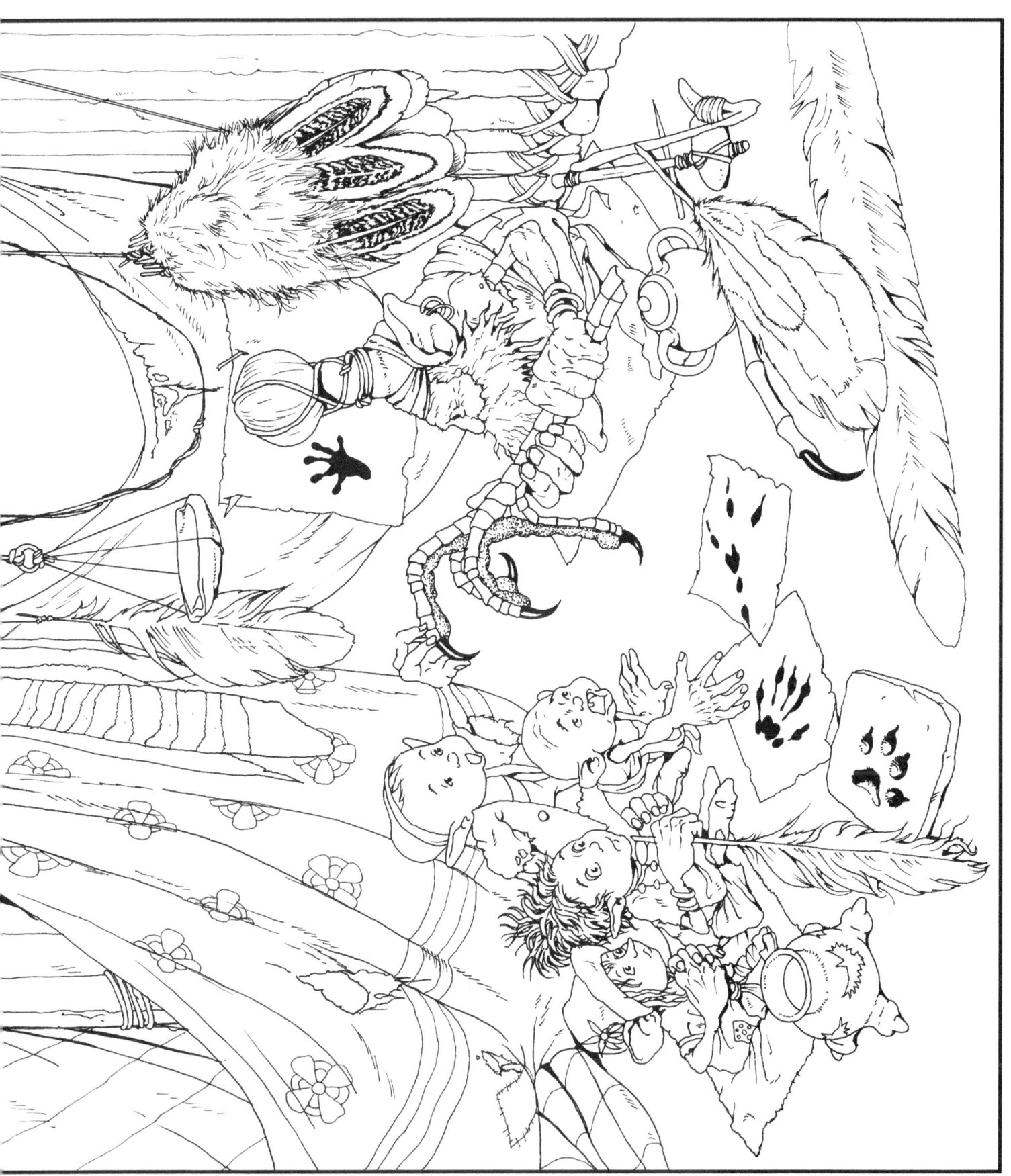

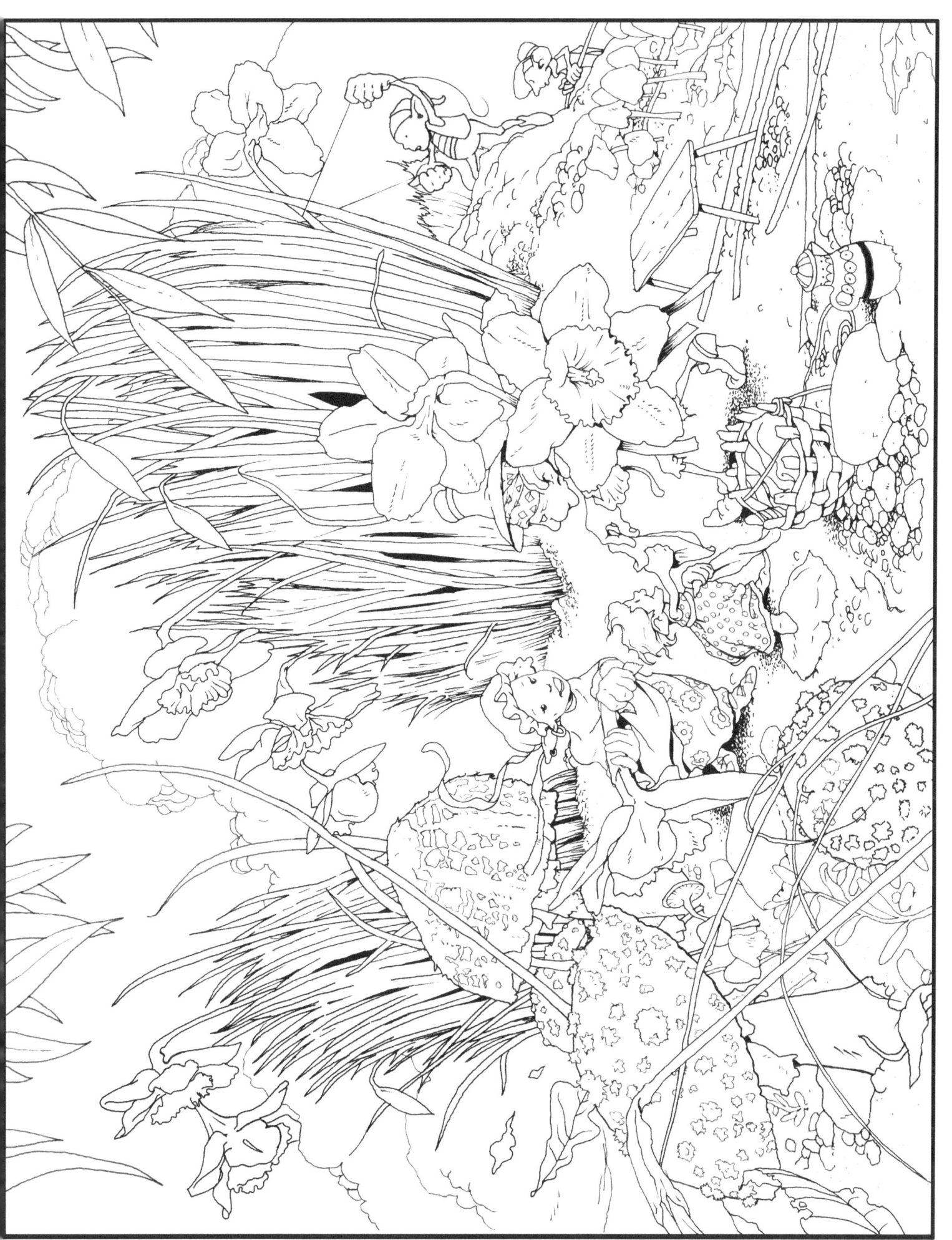

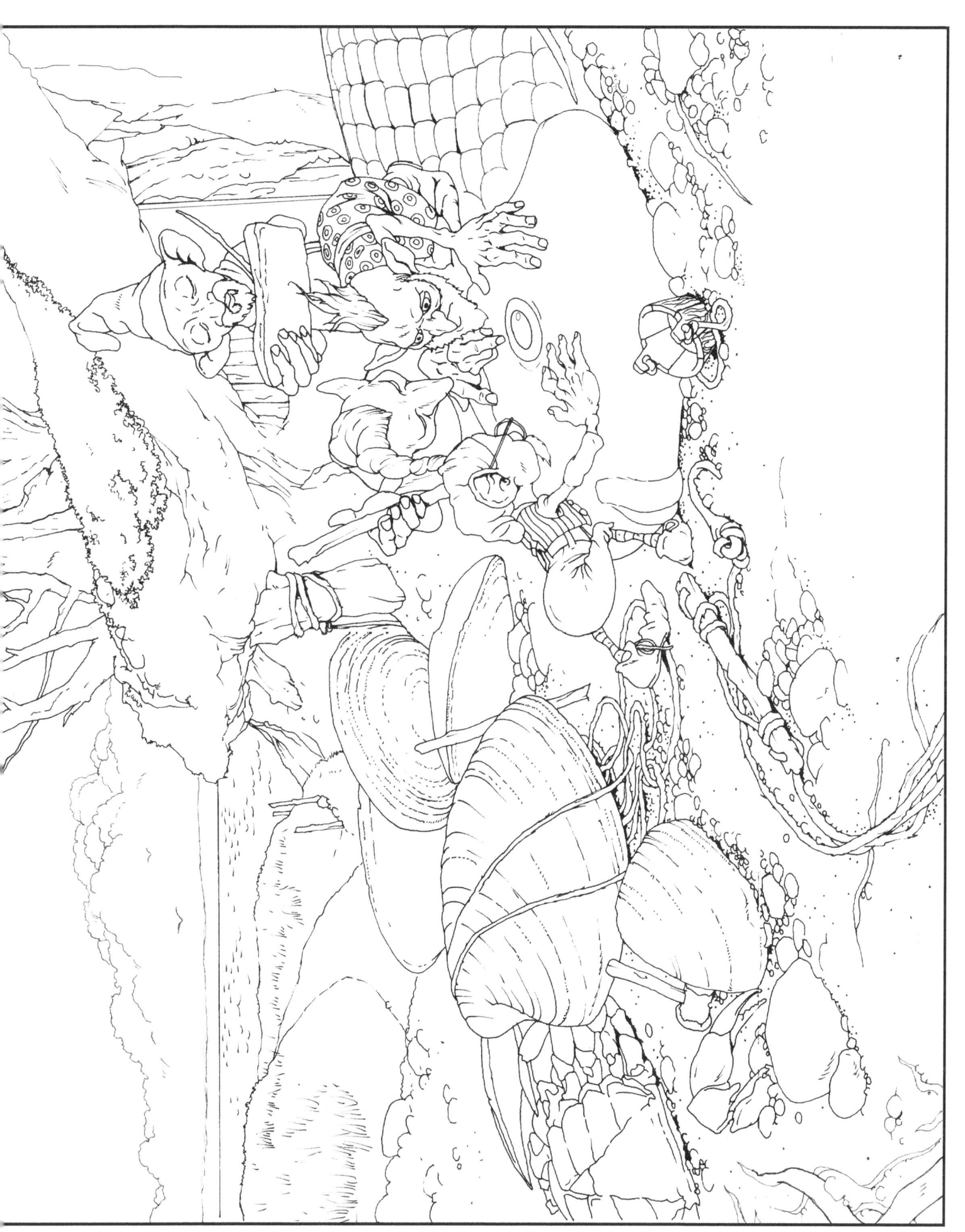

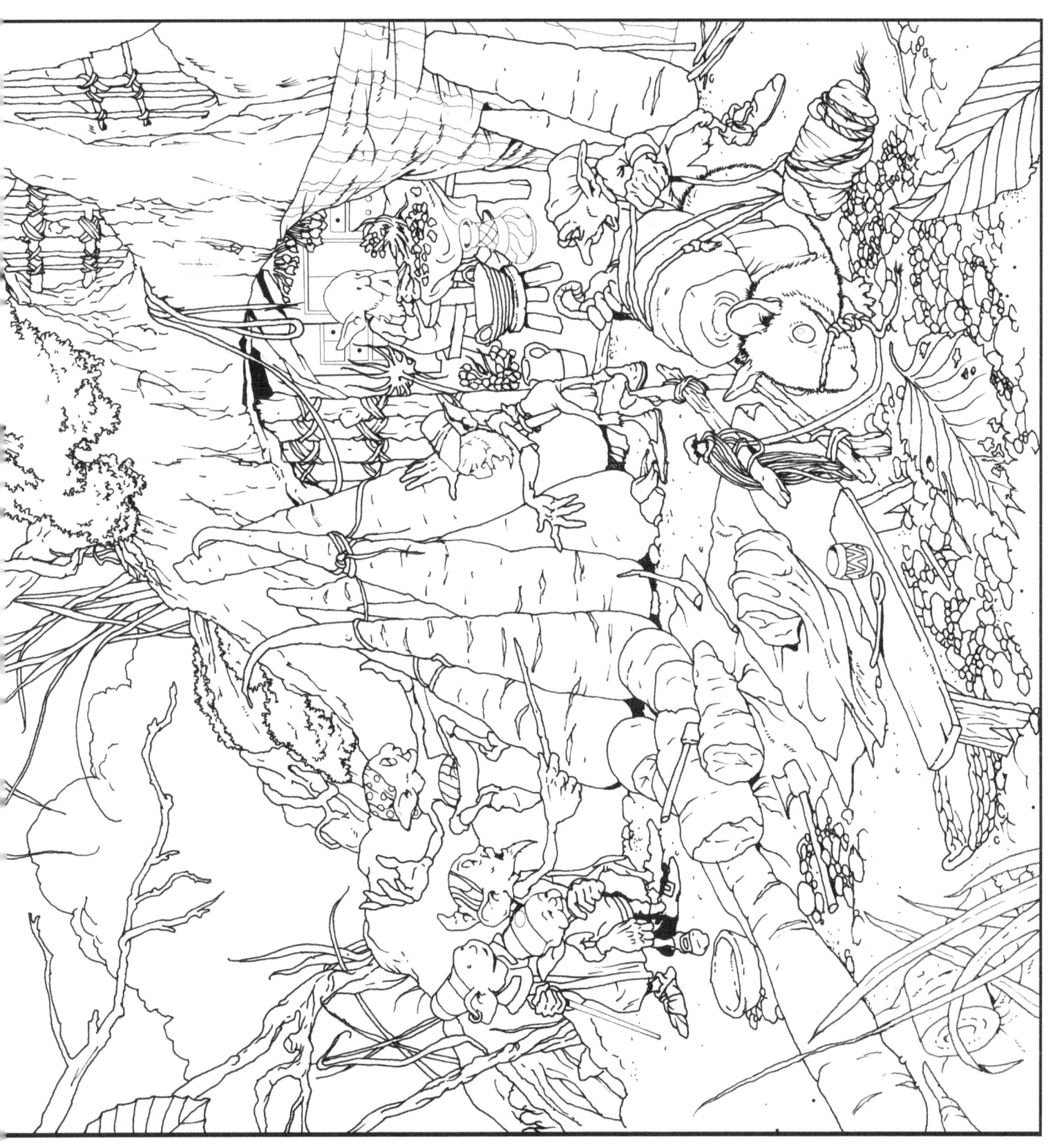

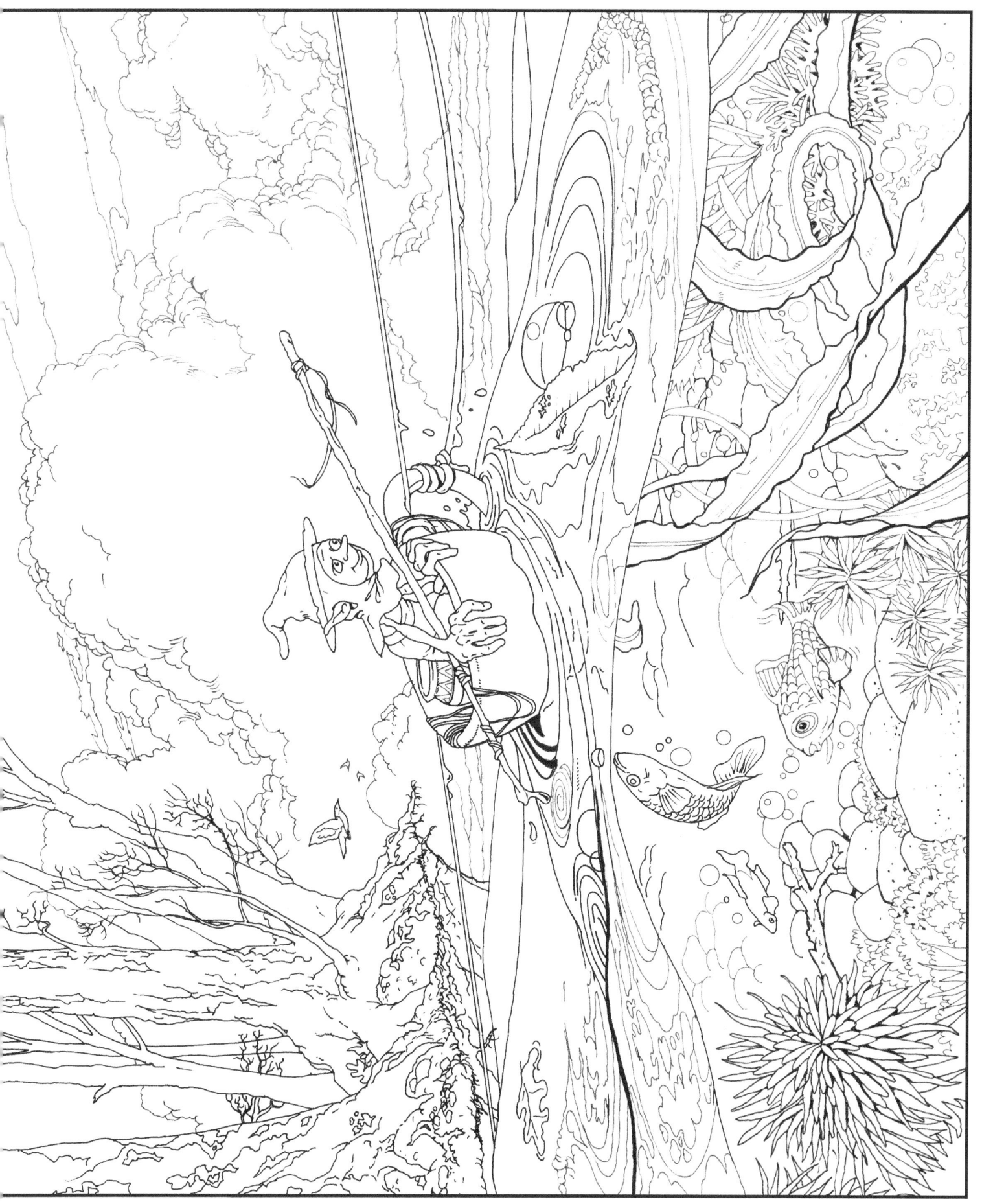

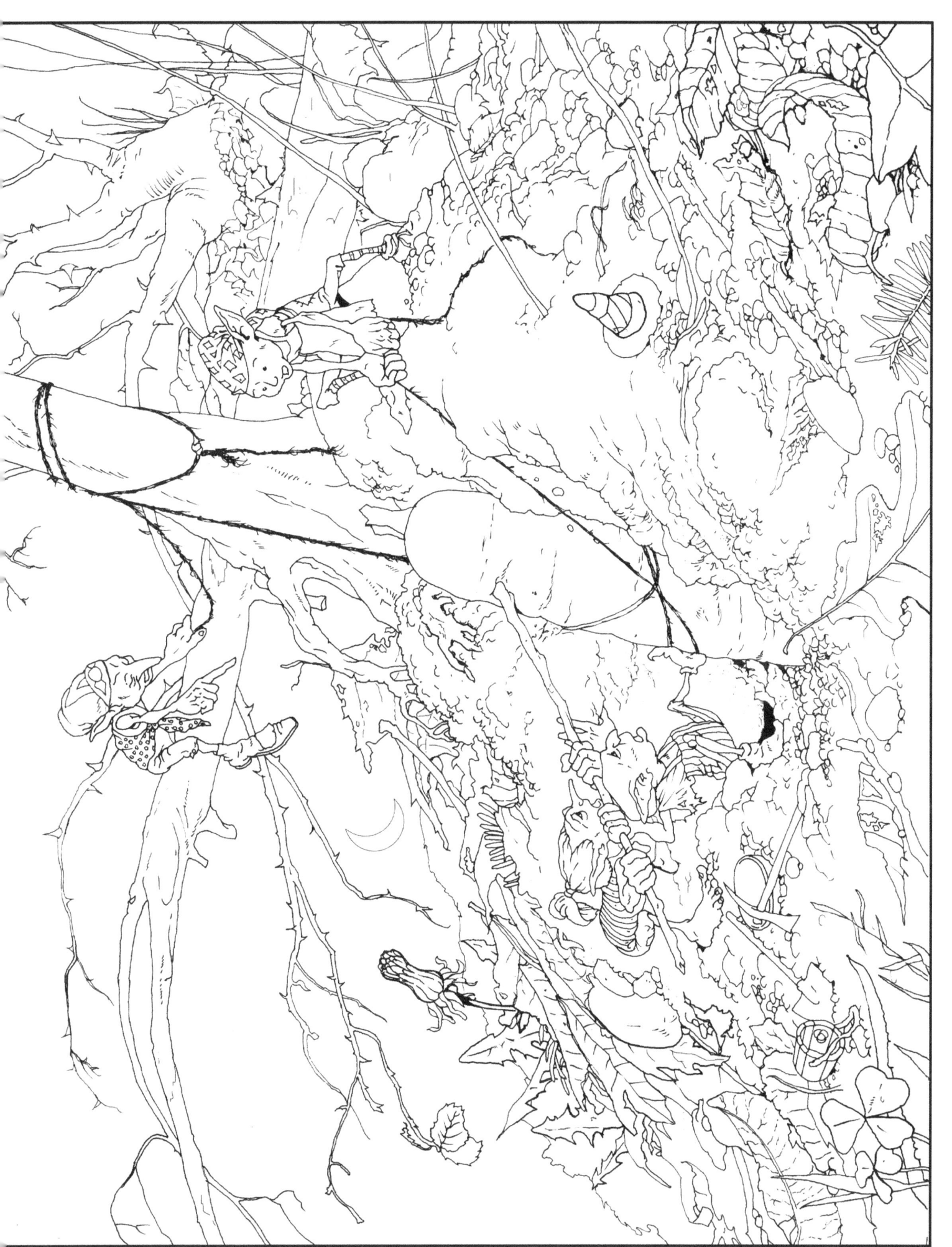

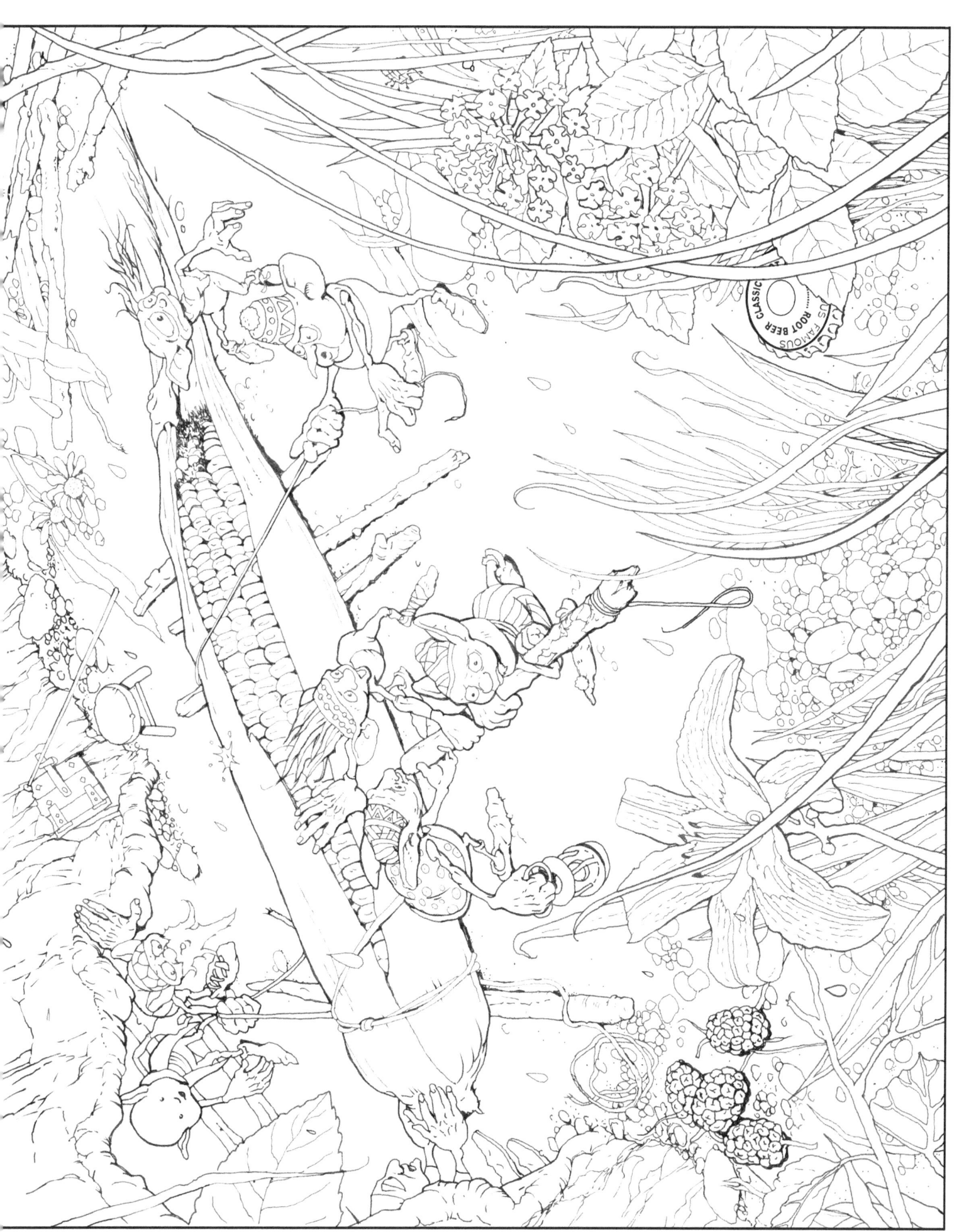

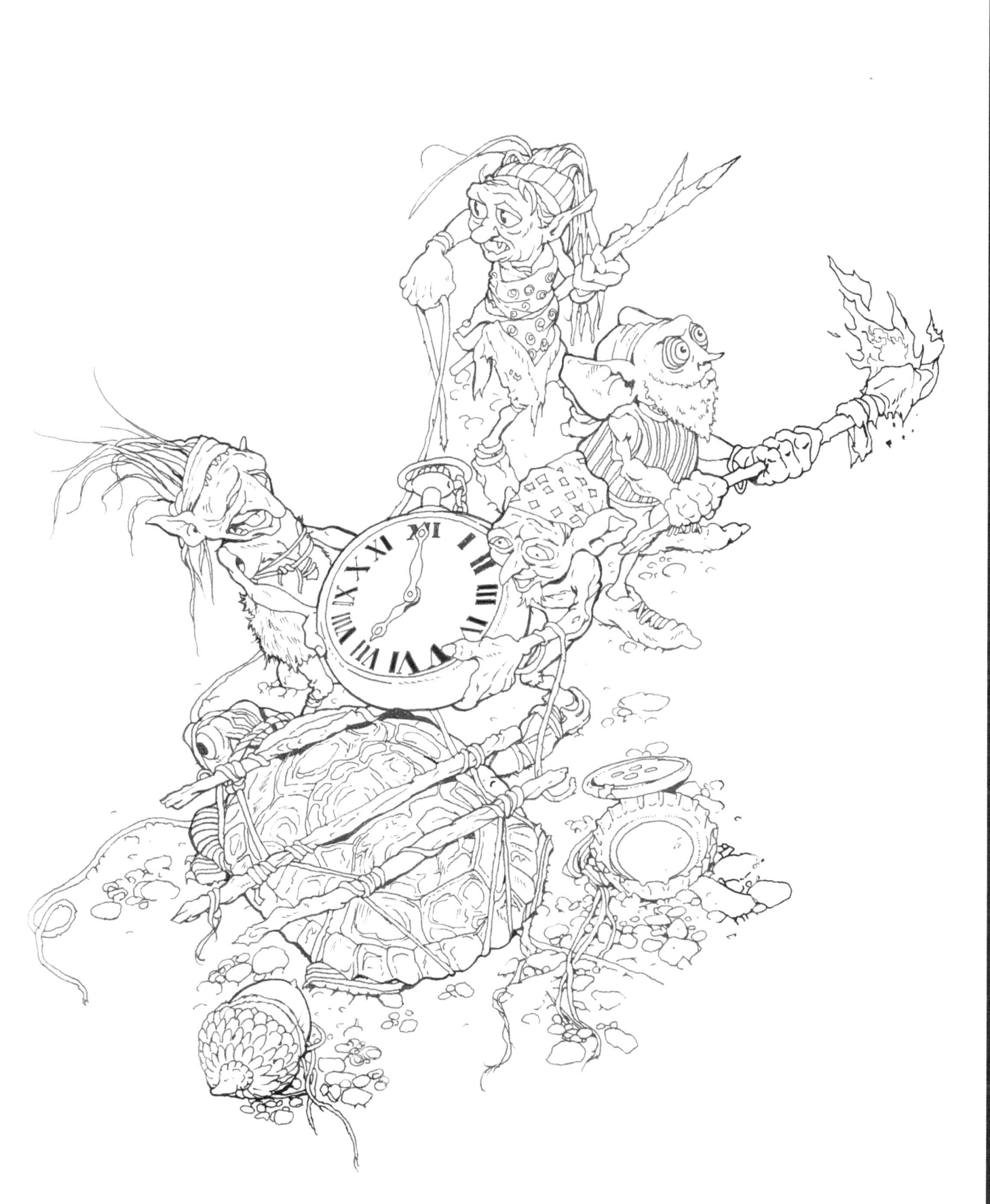

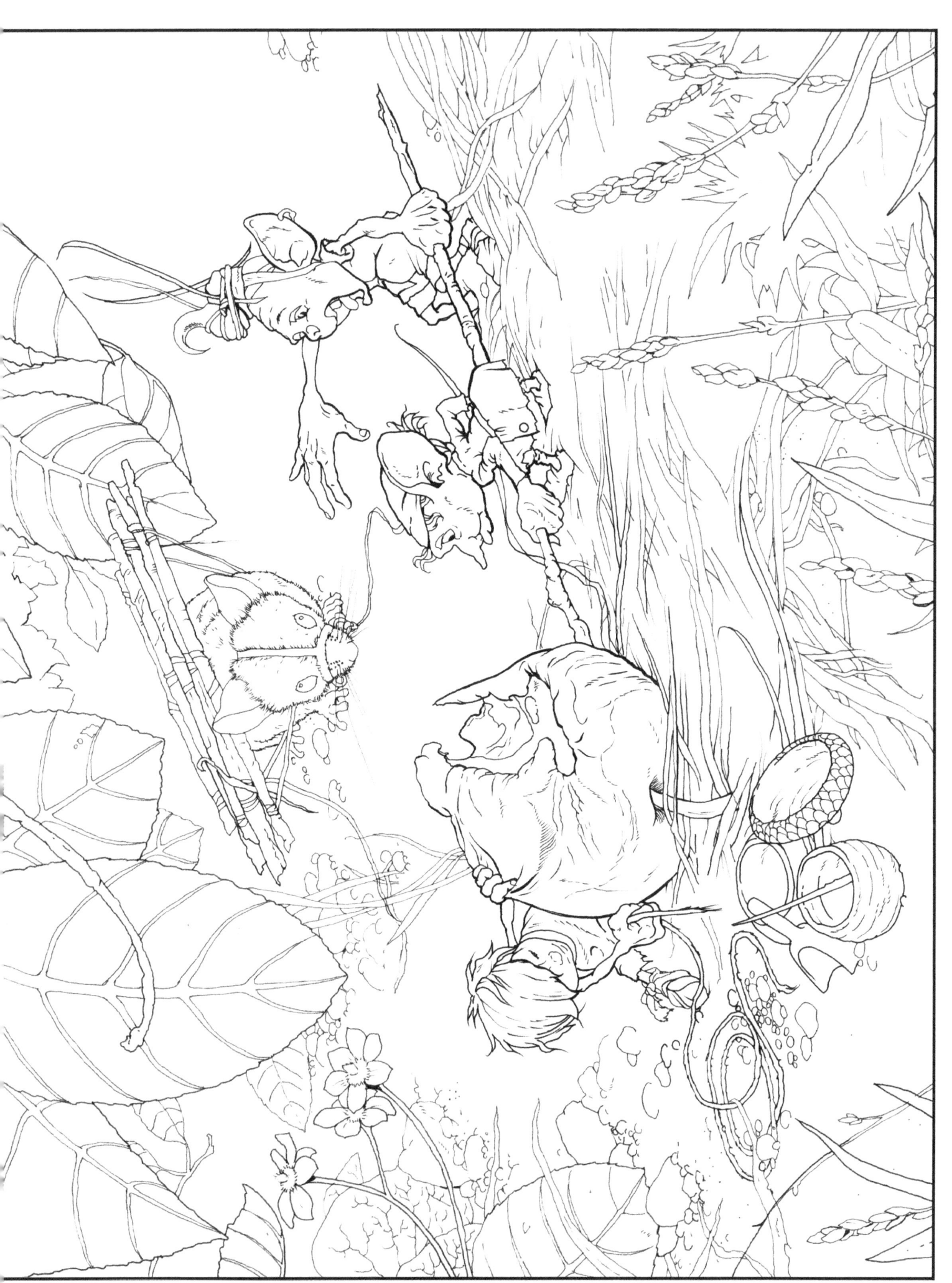

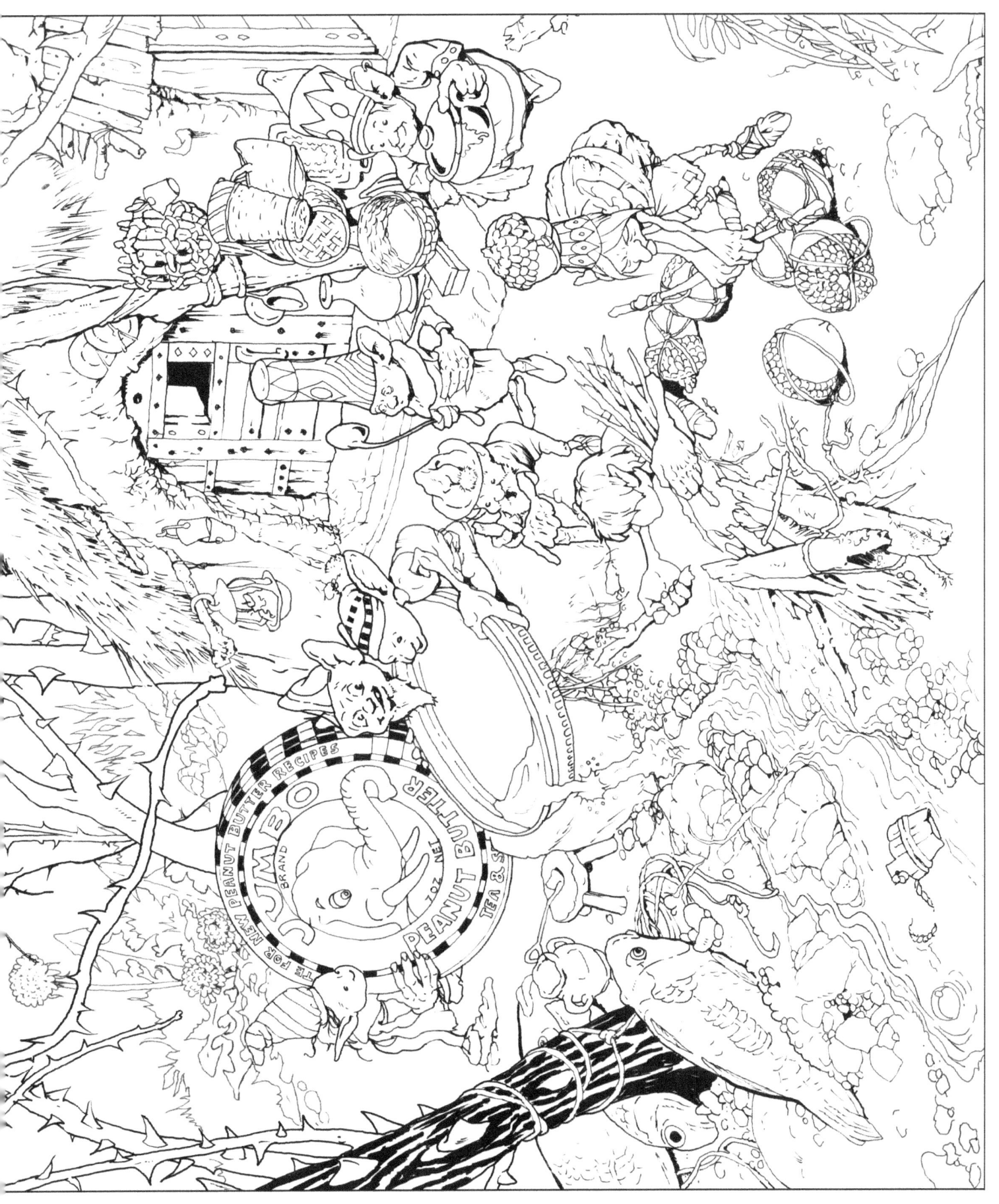

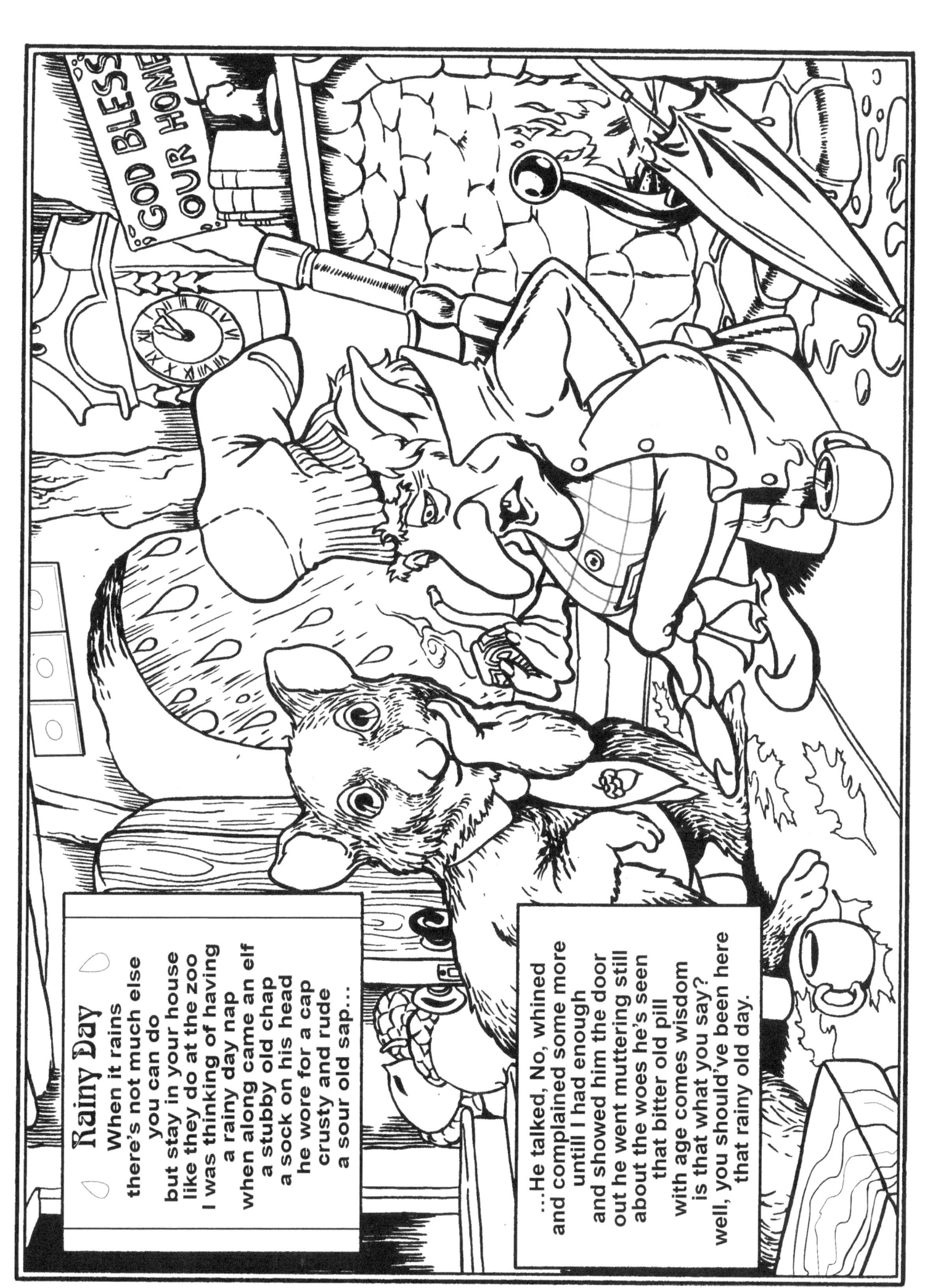

Rainy Day

When it rains
there's not much else
you can do
but stay in your house
like they do at the zoo
I was thinking of having
a rainy day nap
when along came an elf
a stubby old chap
a sock on his head
he wore for a cap
crusty and rude
a sour old sap...

...He talked, No, whined
and complained some more
untill I had enough
and showed him the door
out he went muttering still
about the woes he's seen
that bitter old pill
with age comes wisdom
is that what you say?
well, you should've been here
that rainy old day.

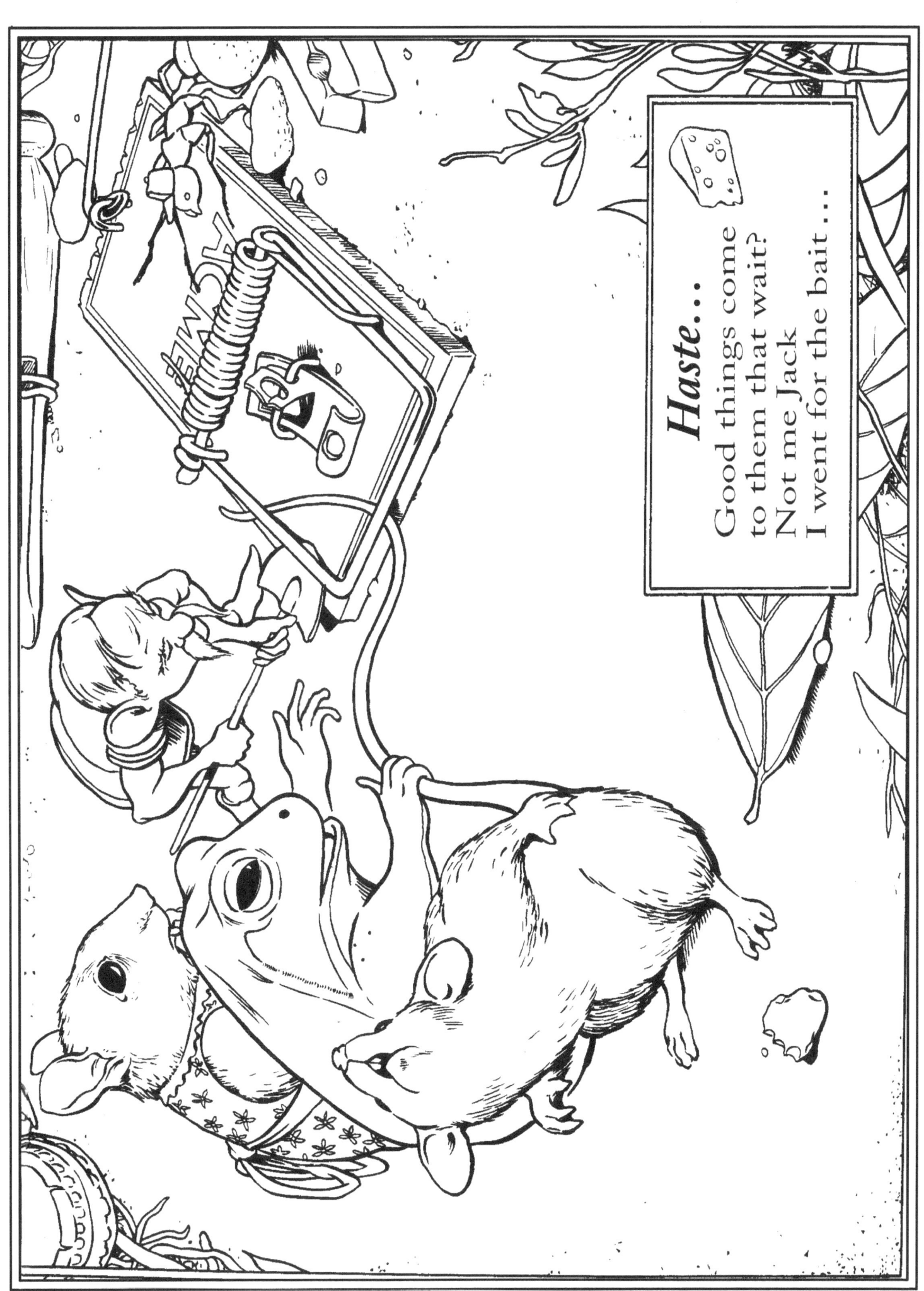

Haste...

Good things come
to them that wait?
Not me Jack
I went for the bait...

www.ingramcontent.com/pod-product-compliance
Lightning Source LLC
Chambersburg PA
CBHW080625180526
45168CB00007B/3059